2007

Christmas in AUSTRIA and Its Capital, VIENNA

A Christmas tree sparkles near Helbling House in Innsbruck, Austria.

Christmas in AUSTRIA and Its Capital, VIENNA

Christmas Around the World from World Book

World Book, Inc.
a Scott Fetzer company
Chicago

Staff

Editorial

*Vice President and
Editor in Chief*
Paul A. Kobasa

*Associate Director,
Supplementary Publications*
Scott Thomas

*Managing Editor,
Supplementary Publications*
Barbara Mayes

Associate Editor
John Stowe

Contributing Editor
Kristina Vaicikonis

Permissions Editor
Janet Peterson

*Manager, Research
Supplementary Publications*
Cheryl Graham

Manager, Indexing
David Pofelski

Graphics and Design

Associate Director
Sandra M. Dyrlund

Senior Designer
Don Di Sante

*Manager, Cartographic
Services*
Wayne K. Pichler

Photographs Editor
Kathy Creech

*Coordinator, Graphics
and Design*
John Whitney

Marketing

Chief Marketing Officer
Patricia Ginnis

Director, Direct Marketing
Mark R. Willy

Marketing Analyst
Zofia Kulik

*Marketing and Print
Promotions Manager*
Marco Morales

Production

*Director, Manufacturing
and Prepress*
Carma Fazio

Manager, Manufacturing
Steven Hueppchen

*Production Technology
Manager*
Anne Fritzinger

Proofreader
Tina Ramirez

Text Processing
Curley Hunter
Gwendolyn Johnson

World Book Inc.
233 N. Michigan Ave.
Chicago, IL 60601

For information about other World Book publications, visit our Web site at **www.worldbook.com** or call **1-800-WORLDBK (967-5325)**. For information about sales to schools and libraries, call, **1-800-975-3250 (United States)**, or **1-800-837-5365 (Canada)**.

Library of Congress Cataloging-in-Publication Data

Christmas in Austria and its capital, Vienna.
    p. cm. -- (Christmas around the world from World Book)
    Summary: "Customs and traditions of the Christmas holidays as celebrated in Austria and its capital, Vienna. Includes crafts, recipes, and carols"--Provided by publisher.
    ISBN 978-0-7166-0810-3
    1. Christmas--Austria. 2. Christmas--Austria--Vienna. 3. Vienna (Austria)--Social life and customs. 4. Austria--Social life and customs. I. World Book, Inc.
GT4987.47.C47 2008
394.266309436--dc22
                                    2007029307

Printed in the United States of America

1 2 3 4 5 6 7 8 9 10 09 08 07

Contents

A Christmas market in the Austrian city of Salzburg entices shoppers with festive lights, colorful decorations and gifts, and aromatic foods.

Awaiting Christkindl

The *Christkindl*, the Christ child, lies at the heart of Christmas in Austria. In other countries, Father Christmas, Saint Nicholas, or Santa Claus may fill the thoughts of children as the Christmas holidays approach. But in Austria, the Christkindl is the star of the season. It is He who brings the children their presents on Christmas Eve. The Christkindl also decorates the tree. His arrival is prepared for and celebrated with deep devotion.

One of the first signs that Christmas and the Christkindl are on their way is the appearance of the *Christkindlmarkt*, or Christmas market. In mid-November, these Christmas markets open in towns and cities all over Austria. The markets may be indoors or outdoors, with rows of booths and stalls selling Advent wreaths, candles, Christmas trees, gingerbread, toys, colorful ornaments and decorations, and small gifts. In larger towns and cities, the Christkindlmarkt is set up in the main square. Rows of booths often fill the entire square, attracting Christmas shoppers from both within the city and outlying districts.

To wander through a Christkindlmarkt is a feast for the senses. Christmas ornaments are abundant in a variety of colors, shapes, and textures. Straw angels smile kindly upon hand-carved wooden shepherds and wise men. Strings of colored glass beads glitter next to boxes of large glass ornaments decorated with silver and gold sparkles. Star-shaped wax molds dangle from cross beams, each with a picture of the Christkindl in the center.

It is not unusual to find craftspeople at work in some of the booths. Shoppers may watch a candlemaker apply the finishing touches to a multicolored Christmas candle. Across the aisle, an artist paints a detailed design on a hand-carved angel's wing. Children wander among the stalls, carefully eyeing the dolls, games, and other toys on display, seeking the perfect present to request from the Christkindl.

Austria's civil flag has stripes of red, white, and red.

In the square, free concerts invite shoppers and vendors to enter into the Christmas spirit. Shoppers can take a rest while they listen to choirs singing Christmas carols and other music of the season.

It is easy to work up an appetite at a Christkindlmarkt, especially when vendors offer pretzels, sausages, and paper cones filled with roasted chestnuts for snacking. Other booths sell cakes, Christmas candies, and gingerbread cookies.

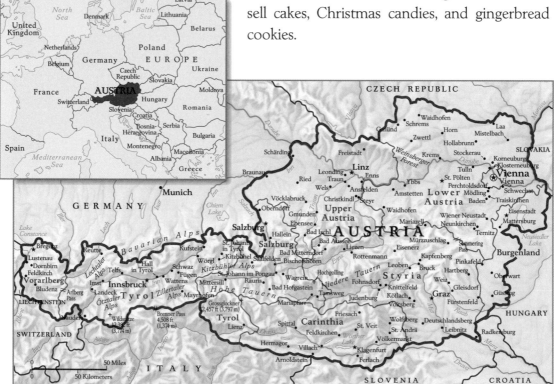

The approach of Christmas in Austria, however, is also a time of thoughtful preparation for celebrating the birth of Jesus. Most people in Austria are Roman Catholics, and many people in Austria observe Advent as a solemn season of preparation for Christmas, similar to Lent, which is the spiritual preparation for Easter. The Advent season marks the beginning of the Christian church year. Advent starts on the Sunday nearest November 30, which is the feast of Saint Andrew. Advent includes the four Sundays before Christmas. The Advent season reminds Christians of the coming of the Christ child.

As the first Sunday in Advent approaches, many families make or purchase an *Adventkranz,* or Advent wreath. It is most often placed

Shoppers linger near a booth selling ornaments and wreaths at a Christkindlmarkt (Christmas market) in Vienna.

on a table, though it may be suspended from the ceiling with strong ribbon. Usually constructed from evergreen boughs, Advent wreaths come in a variety of sizes, some as large as 2 feet (61 centimeters) in diameter. They are decorated with four candles, one for each Sunday in Advent. Usually, three of the candles are purple, and the fourth one is pink, symbolizing joy. Sometimes a larger white candle is placed in the center of the wreath, symbolizing Christ, the Light of the World.

At dusk on the first Sunday of Advent, the family may gather around the wreath to light a single candle and perhaps sing Advent songs or say an Advent prayer. On the second Sunday, two candles are lit; on the third Sunday, three. Then on Golden Sunday—the last Sunday before Christmas—all four candles are set aglow.

Advent calendars help to build a sense of expectation in many Austrian homes. The Advent calendar may picture a mountain village scene, a house with many windows, or perhaps a kind of Jacob's ladder, like the ladder to heaven that Jacob saw in a dream. Every morning, beginning on December 1, children open one little window on the calendar or "climb" a step on the ladder. Behind each window or step appears an angel, a star, or some other picture appropriate to the season. On Christmas Eve, December 24, the last window is opened to reveal the Christkindl smiling up from the manger.

Advent has special songs that are unique to the season. "Blessed Mother of the Savior," "O Come, O Come, Emmanuel," and "Maria Wanders Through the Thorn"—these and other lovely melodies are

A heart-shaped Christmas cookie is one of many tempting treats for sale at Christkindl-markts.

sung and played to prepare for the Christkindl's arrival. Advent songs commonly combine themes of repentance and joyous expectation of the coming of the Christ child.

Singing and musical performances play a significant role in Advent observances, as they do in most other important occasions in this music-loving country. Some schoolteachers set aside classroom time to practice Advent songs. All over Austria, both children and adults often dress in traditional costumes to celebrate the Advent season in song and dance.

Children sing around an Advent wreath with four burning candles— one for each Sunday in Advent— during the week before Christmas.

The *Herbergsuchen,* meaning *seeking shelter,* is a well-established Austrian custom, which is especially popular in the Salzburg and Styria provinces. There are many local variations of the tradition, which often are practiced on behalf of charity. Children go from door to door, enacting Mary and Joseph's search for a place to stay in Bethlehem, and collect money for charity. Sometimes schools or youth groups give performances based on this theme and charge admission. They then donate the proceeds to a worthy cause.

When practiced at home, the custom may center on a treasured religious picture, including those of the Annunciation, the flight into Egypt, or Mary and Joseph's search for a room in Bethlehem. The picture is hung in a certain room in the house and decorated with evergreens and artificial flowers. For nine evenings before Christmas Eve, the family prays and sings Advent songs in front of the picture. Then the picture is mounted on a small portable platform and carried around the house—or from house to house—by the children. Each evening they perform the scene in which Mary and Joseph stand before the closed door of the inn, asking the innkeeper for a place to stay. Then they sing "*Wer klopfet an?*"—the traditional song for the Herbergsuchen.

Wer Klopfet an?
Who's knocking at my door?

Two people poor and low.
What are you asking for?
That you may mercy show.
We are, O Sir, in sorry plight,
O grant us shelter here tonight.
You ask in vain.
We beg a place to rest.
It's "no" again!
You will be greatly blessed.
I told you no!
You cannot stay,
Get out of here and go your way.

Another version of this custom, known as the *Frauentragen,* takes place in Oberndorf, near the city of Salzburg. Young girls carry the image of Mary from house to house. Bearing lanterns and candles, they knock at each door and announce: "The heavenly mother is looking for a place to stay." At each house, money is donated to help the needy during the Christmas season.

December 4 is the feast of Saint Barbara, the patron saint of miners. Workers in the gold mines at Rauris, in the Salzburg province, celebrate the day with "Barbara bread," a special gingerbread roll. At night, they leave out food for the *Bergmannl,* or little people.

All over Austria, "Barbara branches" are cut from cherry or pear trees, brought into houses, and placed in water on December 4. The indoor warmth creates a sort of artificial spring, and the branches come to life. One myth holds that the owner of the first branch to sprout a shoot can look forward to good luck in the coming year. There is another old belief that a person whose Barbara branch blossoms on Christmas Day can expect to be married during the following year.

December 5, St. Nicholas Eve, is known as Krampus Day in some rural areas. Krampus is an evil spirit, or minor devil, that often is covered in frightening fur. He has a long tail and a long red tongue and carries a rattling chain, birch branches, and a big black bag. On Krampus Day, children and adults go together to the village square to throw snowballs at this menacing figure and otherwise try to chase him off. One or more "Krampuses" lie in wait, rattling chains and threatening to carry off naughty children in the big black bags or to punish the children with birch branches. But this is all done in fun, with much teasing and poking and laughter. Krampus's purpose is simply to remind children to be good, and he is especially careful not to actually frighten the younger children.

Saint Nicholas, the special saint of children, is widely honored throughout Austria. He is an ancestor of Santa Claus and Father Christmas, but in Austria, as in many other countries, he appears on his saint's day, a holiday separate from Christmas. In some parts of the country, he makes his appearance on St. Nicholas Eve, December 5, accompanied by Krampus. In other districts, the pair waits until December 6, the feast day of Saint Nicholas, to appear. Occasionally, the saint makes a solo visit. Sometimes he is not seen at all, but the children always know when he has been there. On St.

Nicholas Eve, they place their shoes either on the windowsill or outside their bedroom doors. Saint Nicholas traditionally rewards children who have been good all year by filling their shoes with fruits, nuts, and sweets.

The historical Saint Nicholas was an early Christian martyr and bishop of Myra in Asia Minor in the A.D. 300's. He is said to have saved three young girls from slavery by secretly giving each a bag of gold for her *dowry,* which is money or property that a bride's family gives to the groom when the couple marry. God rewarded the bishop's generosity by giving him permission to walk on Earth on his feast day, bringing gifts to all good children.

In Austria today, Saint Nicholas customarily appears in a flowing robe and *miter*—the tall, pointed headdress

Saint Nicholas and Krampus, an evil spirit carrying birch sticks to punish naughty children, decorate the cover of a Viennese Christmas card.

worn by bishops. He carries a shepherd's staff and a thick book, in which the guardian angels have been keeping track all year of the good and bad deeds of the world's children. That is why he has such astonishing knowledge of each family he visits.

At the appointed time, the whole family, often including grandparents, gathers to await Saint Nicholas's arrival. In he walks, accompanied by Krampus, who is there to deal with the children who deserve a scolding. Saint Nicholas—usually portrayed by a friend, neighbor, or relative—calls each young member of the household forward. He may ask them to give an account of themselves or, perhaps, to recite their prayers. When Krampus attempts to punish the naughty children, Saint Nicholas drives him away. After each child promises to be on his or her best behavior, Saint Nicholas distributes the treats. In addition to nuts, oranges, and sweets, he sometimes rewards good children with birch branches decorated with candy, perhaps to remind them that Krampus is lurking about should they falter.

December 5 traditionally is the day when many Austrian households begin to "smell like Christmas." A special kind of cookie, known as *Speculatius* or *Speculaas,* is baked for St. Nicholas Day. The dough is rolled very thin and then cut in the shapes of Saint Nicholas and Krampus. Saint-shaped cookies are decorated with icing of different colors and candied fruit. Krampus cookies may have raisin eyes, an almond nose, and a red crepe-paper tongue.

For St. Nicholas Day, bakery windows display bread baked in the shape of Krampus and Saint Nicholas. Round sandwiches may also bear the faces of Krampus and Saint Nicholas. The windows are often decorated with birch branches—reminders of the whip with which Krampus threatens naughty children.

Of all his public appearances, Saint Nicholas's official visit to the city of Innsbruck may be the most spectacular. A huge tree sits in the Old Town square before the famous Golden Roof—a late-Gothic bay window with hundreds of gold-plated tiles. The Golden Roof was built in 1500 as a royal box from which Emperor Maximilian I could view entertainment in the square below. Surrounded by children dressed as angels, shepherds, and torchbearers, Saint Nicholas delivers a message of good will to the mayor of Innsbruck. Then he lights the town's Christmas tree in preparation for the Christ child's arrival.

Saint Nicholas greets a child during Christmas celebrations in the city of Salzburg.

December 13, St. Lucy Day, is celebrated mainly in the Lower Austria and Burgenland provinces. On St. Lucy Eve, witches are supposed to possess extraordinary powers. Householders protect themselves against the witches' black magic by purifying their homes with blackthorn and clouds of incense.

On St. Thomas Day, December 21, the entire house is blessed and purified with incense, especially the sleeping quarters. In some areas, farm buildings also are blessed. According to legend, unmarried girls can see into the future on St. Thomas Night—but not without effort. They must first climb into bed over a stool and throw their shoes toward the door, toes pointing toward the door. Then, if they sleep with their heads at the foot of the bed, their dreams will reward them with visions of their future husband. The single woman who can pick out a young rooster from among a brood of sleeping chicks on St. Thomas Day will soon acquire a husband or see him in her dreams.

Throughout the Austrian Alps, St. Thomas Day is the day for baking *Kletzenbrot* and many other traditional Christmas treats. Though it takes its name from the Tyrolean word for *dried pears,* Kletzenbrot actually contains a variety of dried fruits and nuts. This wholesome bread keeps for weeks and seems to improve with age. A large loaf may be baked for the family's breakfast on Christmas morning. Sometimes smaller loaves may be baked for each person in the household.

On St. Thomas Day, the Christmas baking begins in earnest. From then on the house is filled with the appetizing scents of *Lebkuchen, Pfeffernüsse, Stollen,* and the many other delicacies for which the people of Austria are famous.

Amid the many Advent activities and adult preparations, the children are busily making some plans of their own. The Christkindl is much in their thoughts, for it is He who will bring the new bicycles, dolls, games, toys, or other delights that they will receive on Christmas Eve.

Traditionally, Austrian youngsters write to the Christkindl early in Advent to tell Him of their hearts' desires. The Christmas wish list is carefully placed in a window or on a windowsill where the Christ child or one of His angel helpers will be sure to see it. By the following morning, the letter is always gone.

A modern variant of this old custom has grown up in the past few decades, centered in the town of Christkindl. For a small village with fewer than a hundred houses, Christkindl has a fascinating history. It goes back to the late 1600's, when Ferdinand Sertl, variously described as an organist, watchman, and "poor young woodcutter," suffered from epilepsy and other diseases.

In 1695, nuns from a convent near Steyr took pity on Sertl and gave him a small wax statue of the infant Jesus. Sertl took the statue into the woods above Steyr, carved a niche in a big spruce tree, and placed his treasure in the niche.

A child places a Christmas wish list in a window for the Christkindl *(Christ child) or one of His angels to find.*

Every week Sertl climbed the steep, narrow path to the top of the hill to pray at his shrine for relief from his sickness. His perseverance was rewarded. Sertl's illnesses gradually became less severe, until finally they disappeared entirely.

The nuns who donated the statue for Sertl's shrine were duly impressed and lost little time in spreading word of the miraculous cure. Soon pilgrims began to visit the shrine to "the Christ child under the heavens."

As early as 1697, an enclosure was built around the tree. In 1703, the bishop of Passau ordered a church to be built on the site. The cornerstone was laid on May 31, 1708, and construction was completed in 1725 under the supervision of architect Jacob Prandtauer. The ornate design, by Carlo Antonio Carlone, incorporates the living tree as the centerpiece of the altar. The niche and statue can still be seen today.

Local residents began to build their homes in the glade around the church, and soon a small village developed. What better name for the new community than Christkindl—or *Christkindl Unterhimmel* (Christ child under the heavens), as it is sometimes called.

More than two centuries passed relatively uneventfully in Christkindl. But in 1950, the Austrian Postal Administration set up its first

During the Christmas season, millions of letters and packages pass through the Postamt *(post office) in the village of Christkindl to receive a special postmark showing the Holy Family under a Christmas star.*

official Christmas post office in temporary headquarters in the bar of the village inn, "At the Sign of the Heavenly View."

That first season, a lone employee handled some 42,000 pieces of Christmas mail. Today, the Christkindl post office—*Postamt Christkindl*—has enlarged its staff. They handle more than two million letters, packages, and requests each year between late November and January 6.

Children address their letters to the Christkindl in care of the Christkindl post office. If a parent encloses a self-addressed reply envelope, the child receives a special Christmas greeting in response. The greeting bears the Christkindl postmark—a stamp showing the Holy Family under the Christmas star.

Letters and packages from all over Austria are routed through the Christkindl post office to receive the special stamp. Postamt Christkindl also gets letters from children throughout the world.

Quite a few of the packages in the Austrian mail at Christmastime emit the wonderful aromas of cookies, pastries, and other baked goods in transit. *Stollen,* a Christmas coffee cake, is a special favorite. In some families, the godmother traditionally sends her godchild a Christmas Stollen as a gift. This dry, cakelike bread is often gift-wrapped in clear cellophane and tied with a bow of red ribbon. Stollen is usually stored for at least three days before it is eaten, and it keeps well for several weeks. No Austrian Christmas would be complete without it.

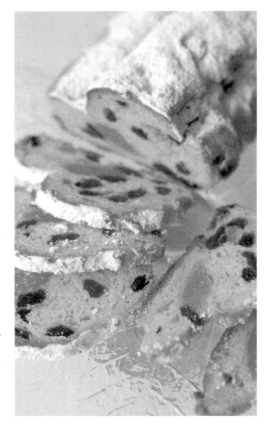

Stollen, *a special type of coffee cake, is a favorite pastry in Austria during Christmas.*

As the Advent season draws to a close, greetings are exchanged, cookies are baked, and other preparations for the Christkindl's arrival proceed with mounting excitement. The tempting odors of Lebkuchen, Pfeffernüsse, Stollen, and other Christmas delicacies drift through city streets and village lanes. Spirits rise like the refrain of one of the most beautiful of all the Advent songs: "*Freue dich, Christkind kommt bald!*" ("Rejoice, for the Christ child is coming soon!")

An Austrian family trudges through a snowy forest with a tree that will be decorated to honor the Christ child's birthday.

An Austrian Family Christmas

Christmas in Austria, more than any other time of year, is a holiday celebrated by and for families. Outside, it is almost always cold, often with snow covering the ground. But inside, Austrian homes radiate the special warmth of the season. Family members who do not see one another at other times of the year make a special effort to get together over the Christmas holidays. *Weihnachtszeit*–Christmastime– is a festive time for youngsters and adults alike.

During the weeks before Christmas, Austrian streets and shop windows, from the largest cities to the tiniest villages, are decorated with evergreens and twinkling colored lights. Bakeries, department stores, toyshops, and other establishments often set up special Christmas displays.

Most Austrian communities erect a big public *Weihnachtsbaum* (Christmas tree) in the main square or some other central location and decorate it with strings of electric lights and ornaments. Small villages often compete to see which has the best tree. Evergreens in public parks may be hung with birdseed or breadcrumb decorations, much to the delight of the birds of the community. Christmas trees can also be found in coffee houses, hotels, railway station waiting rooms, restaurants, theater lobbies, and many other public places.

The lovely custom of lighting and decorating small trees at Christmastime seems to have originated in Germany. One legend traces it to the Middle Ages—a period of time from about the 400's through the 1400's—when Paradise Plays were performed on December 24. The plays reenacted the story of Adam and Eve in the Garden of Eden, and fir trees were decorated with apples to symbolize the tree of knowledge. Yet another tradition attributes the Weihnachtsbaum to Martin Luther, the leader of the Reformation—a religious movement that led to the birth of Protestantism, in about 1530. Luther is said to have used a candlelit tree to remind his followers of the starry heavens on Christmas Eve.

The first Christmas tree for which there is historical evidence is described in a 1605 diary kept by an anonymous visitor to Strasbourg, France, then a town in Germany. The author writes of fir trees set up in parlors and decorated with apples, candies, flat wafers, sugar, and paper roses in a variety of shades. The rose was frequently used in early Christian art as a symbol of the Virgin Mary. The flat wafers are comparable to communion wafers, which are used during Mass. In Austria, a tree hung with such wafers, or with cookies decorated with religious designs, came to be known as a *Christbaum*. The practice of erecting a Christbaum to honor the Christ child's birthday spread throughout Austria during the early 1600's.

The Christbaum also appeared in other forms in the 1600's and 1700's. In some parts of Austria, people cut the tips from large evergreens and hung them upside down in living room or parlor corners, often decorated with apples, candied nuts, and red paper strips. The corner was referred to as "the Lord God's corner." Still another custom was to hang the evergreen tips in windows or from ceiling rafters, right side up. The stem was sharpened to a point, from which an apple was suspended.

For several generations, the Christbaum seems to have existed side by side with a candlelit construction called a *Lichstock*. Evergreen branches were wrapped around open, pyramid-shaped wooden frames and then decorated with candles and pastries. Eventually the candles were transferred to the Christbaum, and the Lichstock became less common.

Although the Christmas tree was fully ornamented and widely accepted throughout Austria by the 1700's, the Austrian royalty did

Austrian parents keep the family Christmas tree secret until Christmas Eve, in keeping with the traditional belief that the Christ child and His angels do most of the decorating.

not adopt the custom until the early part of the 1800's. In 1816, German princess Henrietta von Nassau-Weilburg paid a winter visit to the Austrian royal house of Habsburg. She introduced the Weihnachtsbaum to Emperor Francis I, and from then on the Austrian royal family included a tree in its Christmas celebrations.

Today the Weihnachtsbaum is at the heart of the Austrian family Christmas. In fact, it plays a central role throughout the holiday season. Many children busy themselves near the end of Advent making ornaments for the family Christmas tree—from colored paper, foil, ribbons, straw, or bits and pieces of any other material. They may wrap nuts and candy with foil or tissue paper and attach colored thread so that the Christ child can hang the ornaments easily when He and the angel helpers decorate the Christmas tree. Other materials are fashioned into angels, moons, shooting stars, suns, tiny Christmas trees, trumpets, and more—the only limits are set by the youngsters' imaginations.

In Austria, Christmas is an exciting time for children. School activities reflect the fact that Christmas is the most important holiday of the year. During the last few days before Christmas, school plays that were written and rehearsed earlier in December are finally performed for parents and other relatives and friends. Mothers and fathers, who are busy with their own holiday preparations, may interrupt their work to mend a broken angel's wing or to answer a frantic last-minute plea for help in constructing a cardboard manger.

Most families will make at least one Christmas shopping trip together, perhaps dropping hints about desirable Christmas presents as they gaze in wonder at the many delights displayed in the local Christkindlmarkt and in store windows. Then, of course, the gifts are purchased and wrapped in secret and hidden from the rest of the family until Christmas Eve.

The period just before Christmas Eve is a time of last-minute baking. Homemade gingerbread houses are baked, constructed, and decorated with loving care. *Spanische Windbäckerei,* or Spanish Wind cookies, are another traditional favorite. These meringue cookies, light as the wind, are baked in the shape of little Christmas wreaths and often are used as ornaments for the Weihnachtsbaum.

In some families, the parents go in secret to purchase the Christmas tree, which is kept out of the children's sight until Christmas Eve. Other families go together to the Christmas tree lot, carefully inspecting each evergreen before making a final selection.

Children in Austria do not see the decorated family tree until Christmas Eve. It is kept behind the closed doors of the "Christmas room"—at other times of the year known as the living room or parlor. For several days before the big event, the Christmas room is off-limits to children. The Christ child and His angels are decorating the family tree, with occasional assistance from Mother, Father, or other adults in the family.

Christmas Eve is the traditional time to exchange gifts with friends and family. Shops close by 6 p.m. The curtains drop in concert halls, movie houses, and theaters. Restaurants and nightclubs grow silent and dark. Traffic seems to disappear from the streets.

Most homes in Austria enter the final stages of preparation for Christkindl's arrival. For the children, the excitement is almost unbearable. Adults tiptoe about and communicate in whispers. Mother and Father may spend much of the day wrapping gifts in the Christmas room. Every so often they are interrupted by a quiet knock at the door. They open it to the sound of receding footsteps and look down to find a stack of Christmas presents, each one with a name tag. Parents are not the only ones with Christmas Eve surprises!

Grandparents, uncles, aunts, and cousins often arrive in the early evening. Candles are placed in the windows as a symbolic greeting to absent friends and relatives, and in memory of those who have passed away.

Finally, the children hear the sound they have all been awaiting—the tinkling bell that summons them to the Christmas room. There, for the first time that season, they witness Christkindl's handiwork.

Each year's Weihnachtsbaum seems the most magical ever. Dozens of cookies are tied to the branches with colored thread or ribbon. Small apples and tangerines may dangle from the lower limbs. Decorations often include angels, birds, and other creatures made of wood and straw, or wax stars bearing pictures of the infant Jesus. Christkindl also may appear wrapped in swaddling clothes or even enjoying Himself on a sled. Then there are the children's home-made ornaments and other handcrafted decorations—some, perhaps,

Austria is famous for its delicious Christmas pastries and cookies.

which have been treasured for generations. Silver and gold garlands crisscross the tree like threads of a dew-decked spider's web. Tinsel shines gently from every branch against softly glowing lights.

Almost every family in Austria also has a *Weihnachtskrippe,* or Nativity scene, with miniature figures of the newborn Christ child and His parents. Often the figures are dressed in traditional Austrian costumes. A Weihnachtskrippe may have only a few figures—perhaps the Holy Family, a shepherd or two, and a few animals. But other families display very elaborate scenes, with dozens of animals, hand-carved shepherds, and other figures. Some families keep adding new characters and scenery each year, especially if a family member is a talented woodcarver. Often these mangers are hundreds of years old, treasured heirlooms handed down from one generation to the next.

The Weihnachtskrippe is usually placed under the Christmas tree, next to the presents. It may be set up before Christmas Eve, especially if it is a very detailed Weihnachtskrippe. But Christkindl is not placed in the manger until Christmas Eve.

After the birthday of Christkindl has been recognized, and everyone has had a chance to admire the tree and Weihnachtskrippe, the family members lift their voices in song. One favorite Christmas carol is "Silent Night, Holy Night." Joseph Mohr, a Roman Catholic priest, wrote the words to this beautiful carol in 1816, in the Austrian village of Mariapfarr, southeast of Salzburg. In 1818, Franz Xaver Gruber set the words to music, and it was performed for the first time that Christmas Eve in a church in Oberndorf, a village north of Salzburg. In other countries, this carol may be played on the radio and television, in stores, and in restaurants during the weeks before Christmas. But in Austria, "Silent Night, Holy Night" is heard for the first time on Christmas Eve, and the effect is spellbinding.

Other carols, of folk or classical origin, are also sung with enthusiasm in the family home on Christmas Eve. "Above, on the Mountain," "A Baby in the Cradle," "Still, Still, Still," and "The Twilight Is Falling" may be followed by Christmas poems and readings that have been memorized by the family's younger members. And someone may relate the most important story of all—the story of the Nativity itself.

The adults and children exchange the traditional Christmas greeting: *Fröhliche Weihnachten!* (Merry Christmas!) In some families, members wish one another a blessed Christmas—*Gesegnete Weihnachten.*

Finally, the children are free to turn their attention to the gifts under the tree. Everyone joins in the exchange of presents, the *Bescherung.* Sweaters are tried on for size, games are unwrapped, and the children enjoy their new toys. For the next hour or so, the Christmas room is filled with happy exclamations.

With all this excitement, the whole family has worked up a hearty appetite. The typical Christmas Eve dinner consists of a main course of carp, since the day is traditionally a day for fasting. Along with the fish, the meal usually consists of potato salad, a fish soup, and a variety of cookies or other sweets for dessert. The carp may be baked or broiled or dipped in breadcrumbs, eggs, and flour, and fried in deep fat until golden brown.

A traditional and very popular method is to boil the carp in a broth with vinegar. When boiled in the vinegar, the fish turns blue. More adventurous cooks may prepare Polish-style carp in *aspic* (a type of jelly) or serve the fish cold with a Hungarian paprika sauce. Sometimes the fish is baked in black sauce, especially in families that like Czech-style cooking.

As midnight approaches, it is time to get ready for Mass. In many churches—such as St. Stephen's Cathedral in Vienna, where thousands attend midnight Mass on Christmas Eve—musicians climb to the church towers and trumpet forth Christmas music to call the faithful to worship. The *Turmblasen*—brass instruments playing choral music from the city tower or steeple of the main church—is a traditional feature of Christmas Eve.

Churches lacking trumpeters often send their best carolers to the church towers to guide parishioners on their way to Mass. Rural families will hold torches in their hands as they make their way down from the mountains to attend services in the valley. These long, torchlight processions make Christmas Eve a dramatic and memorable occasion.

Nativity plays and mystery pageants often are performed at Christmastime. In the past, these *Christi-Geburtsspiele* were performed as part of the midnight Mass, and in some rural churches this tradition still exists. Children and adults act out the numerous stories surrounding the birth of Christ. The Annunciation and the Nativity are two common themes. The various shepherds who came to the manger to worship the newborn Christ child are much beloved in Austria, as are the Three Wise Men. Another popular story is that of the Holy Family's flight into Egypt to escape persecution by Herod's soldiers. These folk dramas often are enacted in local dialect by performers wearing traditional Austrian costumes.

As the service comes to a close, the priest blesses his parishioners and sends them out into the early hours of Christmas morning. Crowds of sleepy adults and youngsters make their way home through the Christmas snow. Those who are awake enough may snack on leftover pastries or perhaps enjoy a plate of sausages before retiring. But others dive straight into their beds, exhausted from the day's excitement.

St. Stephen's Cathedral (right in the photo) in central Vienna—named for the city's patron saint—attracts thousands of worshipers for midnight Mass on Christmas Eve.

A horse-drawn sleigh is a common sight during the Christmas season in some parts of Austria.

Christmas Day is one of quiet celebration and happy reunions with family and friends. Some families will attend Mass again on Christmas Day before gathering the family together for the holiday dinner.

As is true of most important occasions in Austria, the Christmas holiday is fueled by a variety of tempting specialties to eat and drink. At breakfast, the family most likely will enjoy the Kletzenbrot baked on St. Thomas Day, December 21, or perhaps a Stollen. Throughout Christmas Day, friends and relatives who come to visit may be offered a glass of wine or a fragrant and potent *Weihnachtspunsch*.

Christmas dinner typically begins with a soup course. This is usually a rich beef broth with tiny dumplings or bits of thin pancakes floating in it. A traditional entrée is roast goose stuffed with apples, prunes, or chestnuts. Other popular alternatives are ham, roast pork, and *Wiener Schnitzel*—the lightly breaded veal cutlet that originated in Austria and is enjoyed around the world. Roasted potatoes and red cabbage or sauerkraut often accompany the main course, with other side dishes of roasted apples, stewed prunes or apricots, and a salad of cabbage or other greens.

For those who can still manage to eat dessert, a variety of temptations are offered. An apple, nut, or poppy seed *strudel* (pastry covered by thin dough) is almost always included. There also might be a cake, a Christmas Stollen, and assorted other pastries and cookies. The dinner is washed down with generous glasses of wine and usually is followed by coffee. After dinner, the Christmas tree is lit again, and almost everyone joins in singing carols.

By the evening of Christmas Day, most of Austria's concert halls, movie houses, nightclubs, and theaters have reopened after their Christmas Eve silence. Many families finish Christmas Day by attending a performance together. Others might leave for a winter ski vacation or for a holiday visit with relatives in another city or town.

December 26, St. Stephen's Day, is a legal holiday from work and school and also a day set aside for visiting. In the streets and squares are crowds of people, many wearing brand-new scarves or sweaters. Many children will be carrying their favorite new toys.

Saint Stephen, the first Christian martyr, is also the patron saint of horses. There are several pageants celebrated in the saint's honor in various parts of Austria, as well as numerous horse shows and races. In the Salzburg area, people still bake bread in the shape of horseshoes to celebrate the day.

The province of Carinthia also has some Saint Stephen's pageants. In Lind, church altars are draped with red cloth for the feast day Mass. The cloth is then cut into pieces, which are distributed after church as good luck charms for horses.

In medieval times, the Twelve Nights after Christmas were a period of rest for domestic animals. The horse, an exceptionally useful four-legged creature, was given a feast day of its own.

Up until World War II (1939-1945), farmers in Austria commonly decorated their horses on St. Stephen's Day, weaving ribbons through the animals' manes and tails. After a solemn High Mass, the priest would bless the animals with holy water. He also blessed the hay and oats used to feed the horses.

Christmas Eve, Christmas Day, and St. Stephen's Day are three feast days that combine to form the most popular holiday season in Austria. Christmas is a time for strengthening family ties, renewing faith, and exchanging tokens of love and appreciation with relatives and friends. It is a holiday with a distinctly religious theme because it celebrates the birth of Jesus. But in Austria, the winter celebrations do not cease on St. Stephen's Eve. In fact, December 26 marks the opening of the magical and mysterious festival of Twelve Nights.

Fireworks light up the sky at many New Year's celebrations in Austria.

Twelve Nights

St. Stephen's Day, December 26, starts the period known as the Twelve Nights, whose activities are a blend of *secular* (nonreligious) and religious traditions. Also called the *Rauhnächte,* or Raw Nights, the period ends on the feast of the Epiphany, January 6, which celebrates the arrival of the Three Wise Men from the East at the stable in Bethlehem. Austria celebrates the New Year with many festivities—much like the rest of the world, but with a distinctly musical twist, as one would expect of a nation with such a brilliant artistic heritage. Vienna plunges into each new year "with music on her lips and in her heart."

The Twelve Nights begins as midnight approaches on Christmas Day, St. Stephen's Eve. According to legend, the animals in their stables begin to look around, anxiously checking out doors and windows to make sure that no one is watching. Once convinced that they are alone, the animals put their heads together and tell each other about their experiences during the past year. They then talk of what the coming year will bring. The gift of speech on St. Stephen's Eve is God's reward to the animals for the burdens they must bear during the rest of the year. In many legends, water turns to wine during this holy night, and treasures can be discovered.

During the dark, stormy Twelve Nights, the one-eyed god Woden is said to gallop through the sky on his eight-legged horse, Sleipnir, leading the Wild Host. One superstition holds that the only way to avoid being kidnapped is to throw oneself into the left track of the road. Woden and his horse are the legendary ancestors of the *Goldenes Roessel,* or the Golden Horse, which in some parts of Austria brought gifts to the children before Saint Nicholas and Christkindl. The Golden Horse generally tried to avoid being seen. But a person who observed a strict fast until noon sometimes could catch a glimpse of the magnificent creature galloping over a rooftop.

In ancient times, the winter solstice marked the beginning of the year. But in 1691, Pope Innocent XII formally declared January 1 to be New Year's Day. In Austria, New Year's Eve is called *Sylvesterabend,* or the Eve of St. Sylvester. The last day of the year is dedicated to the pope who baptized Constantine the Great, the first emperor of the Roman Empire to become a Christian.

As with the Twelve Nights, New Year's celebrations combine religious and secular elements. In earlier times, Austrian taverns and inns were decorated with green plants. A large wreath was hung from the ceiling in the largest room, and a strange character known as Sylvester lurked in a dark corner. Ancient and ugly, Sylvester wore a *flaxen* (pale yellow) beard and a mistletoe wreath on his head. Anyone who passed beneath the evergreen wreath was likely to receive a rough hug and kiss from the old character. But when midnight came around, Sylvester was, like the old year, banished.

New Year's Eve is celebrated with noise and merrymaking. According to tradition, the noise chases away evil spirits along with the old year. *Böllers,* or miniature *mortars* (short-range cannons), are fired, church bells are rung, and trumpets are sounded. In some of the larger cities, people are treated to midnight fireworks displays.

People in Austria believe that a new year should have a positive beginning. Champagne, confetti, and streamers are all part of family celebrations. Pork is a favorite food for New Year's celebrations. The traditional entrée is suckling pig, roasted to perfection. Perhaps this tradition goes back to the ancient custom of sacrificing a wild boar in honor of the new year. It is also said that the pig brings good luck because it moves forward as it creates furrows in the ground with its snout. In the same vein, many people in Austria refuse to eat a crayfish or lobster on New Year's Eve because these creatures move backward.

A few of Vienna's finest restaurants offer an amusing variation of the good-luck pig tradition. On New Year's Eve, chefs or waiters bring a live pig into their elegant dining rooms, and the diners may touch the pig for good luck.

New Year's Eve in Vienna offers a variety of other ways to mark the occasion. Attending midnight Mass at St. Stephen's Cathedral is one of Vienna's traditions. Those who wish to start the year with music may attend the opera or the symphony. The popular Johann Strauss, Jr., operetta *Die Fledermaus* is presented every New Year's Eve and New Year's Day at the Vienna State Opera. On the afternoon of December 31, the Vienna Philharmonic presents an all-Strauss concert of waltzes and polkas. A repeat performance of this concert on New Year's Day is televised throughout Europe and is broadcast in many other countries around the world.

In the countryside, people either go to a restaurant or enjoy New Year's Eve dinner at home. All over Austria, the blowing of trumpets from church towers, a custom also observed on Christmas Eve, signals midnight. People customarily exchange kisses, expressing their feelings of good will. Everyone offers wishes of good health, success, and in the countryside, an abundant harvest.

New Year's Eve marks the beginning of the annual Carnival season, known as *Fasching,* which lasts until the beginning of Lent. All over Austria, gala balls and parties are enjoyed throughout the weeks of Fasching, launched by the Imperial Ball in Vienna on New Year's Eve. The highlight of the Vienna Fasching season is the Opera Ball, held later in February. A favorite treat of the Carnival season is *Faschingskrapfen,* or Carnival jelly doughnuts.

Good luck symbols called *Glücksbinger* are customarily exchanged on New Year's Eve and New Year's Day. Chocolate and *marzipan* (almond and sugar candy) are shaped into chimney sweeps, gold coins, four-leaf clovers, horseshoes, and pigs. In the villages, New Year's morning is usually celebrated by attending Mass. Children go from house to house, singing New Year's songs and offering good wishes. In some places, a choir or band serenades door-to-door.

There is a long-standing belief that everything a person does on January 1 will indicate how the rest of the year will go. If a person is late that day, he or she is likely to be late for many days in the year. A person who sees a chimney sweep first thing in the morning on January 1 is sure to have an excellent year. By contrast, it is a very bad sign if an old woman is the first person one encounters.

Many Austrian New Year's traditions have to do with predicting the future. One sure way of finding out what the coming year will bring is by "pouring lead." Everyone gathers round the fireplace or stove, where lead buttons or pieces of old lead pipe are melted in an iron *ladle* (large, long-handled spoon). The ladle is held over an open fire or candle, and the melted lead is then poured into a bucket of cold water. The lead hardens into all kinds of strange shapes, called *Bleigiessen.*

Every group has at least one *soothsayer*–someone with a skill for interpreting the "lead language." A lump in the shape of a boat, car, or train is a sure sign that someone is about to leave on a journey. A lump shaped like an old woman may bring bad luck, but a heart-shaped lump means the year will be filled with love.

In certain parts of the country, unmarried girls throw their slippers behind them. From the way the slippers fall, the young women can learn whether or not they will be married that year.

As the clamor of New Year's celebrations comes to an end, the merrymaking of the Twelve Nights continues. In earlier times, the nights between Christmas and Epiphany were called "Smoke Nights" because the people went through their houses and barns burning incense and blessing their homesteads. Today, this practice persists in some households on only one night—the last of the Twelve Nights, January 6. The head of the household moves through the house and farm buildings with a pan or shovel full of charcoal, on which incense is burned to smoke out evil spirits. A young member of the family assists in the annual rite by sprinkling holy water over the house, grounds, and barns. After the whole homestead has been blessed, the head of the household marks the *transoms* (strengthening crossbars) of all the doors in chalk, writing the initials thought to be those of the Three Wise Men—K(asper) + M(elchior) + B(althasar)—and the number of the year. These three letters have replaced the pagan *Drudenfuss,* or Druid's foot, which is a pentagram once thought to prevent evil spirits from entering homes.

In rural Austria, the Twelve Nights also is observed with long processions of masked and costumed characters, sometimes blowing horns or cracking whips. These have evolved from ancient purification

Accompanied by an accordion player, men wearing masks and trousers decorated with pompoms celebrate the beginning of Fasching in the town of Patsch.

The Vienna Philharmonic celebrates New Year's Eve and New Year's Day with all-Strauss concerts of polkas and waltzes.

rites, intended to drive away ghosts and evil spirits. In certain areas, they also derive from spring rituals that are centuries older than the Christian feasts they now observe. These processions take various forms in different provinces of Austria, but all are colorful and exciting.

In the Pongau area of the Salzburg province, as in other Alpine provinces, a centuries-old tradition called the *Perchtenlauf* is observed. According to an ancient story, Frau Perchta was a half-man and half-woman creature with supernatural powers. The creature was extremely unpredictable, for its nature was both very good and very evil. Sometimes it travels through the land as a courteous character, bestowing blessings and good wishes. At other times, the creature is ugly and gloomy, with untidy hair and a long, pointed nose. It moves about in a threatening manner, punishing evildoers and bringing misfortune and ruin to all.

In the Perchtenlauf, the various participants, called *Perchten,* are costumed to represent the qualities of Frau Perchta. Because the creature is both good and evil, some of the characters are "good" Perchten and others are "bad" Perchten. All the participants, even those dressed as women, are men and boys from the local area.

Most of the Perchten costumes have been handed down from one generation to the next. The Perchtenlauf costumes are quite complex. The headdresses may be several yards or meters high, and some weigh nearly 80 pounds (36 kilograms). Good Perchten are decorated with bright flowers, Christmas decorations, gold coins, necklaces, and watch chains. They carry dried cow or horse tails, which they use as whips to drive away the evil spirits. They wear wide leather belts around their waists, to which are tied heavy rolls of bells. The loud noise also helps drive away evil spirits. Bad Perchten are dressed like fearsome animals, devils, goblins, and witches. They wear grotesque, wood-carved masks with fangs and horns.

On the eve of the Epiphany, when Frau Perchta traditionally was at her wildest, the parade participants gather at a place known only to them. After a speech by the captain, the parade begins, led by a small band of musicians. At the rear, an animal trainer with a bear on a chain keeps crowds from breaking into the parade.

Farmers and townspeople gladly receive the good Perchten, because they bring best wishes for happiness and fertility. After the

Perchten do a short dance, the homeowners offer them refreshments. Meanwhile the bad Perchten are up on the roof, throwing snowballs, dumping snow down the chimney, and otherwise creating mischief.

Another Perchten is King Herod, who has authority over the whole event. He condemns the bad Perchten to death and orders them bound with chains. But immediately afterward, he reverses his decision, letting the mischief-makers off with a small fine. The Perchtenlauf ends in a spirit of good will.

Another procession known as the *Glöcklerlauf,* or Bell-ringers Parade, takes place in the villages of Styria, a province in eastern Austria. The Glöcklerlauf is held annually on Epiphany Eve, January 5. Records show that the custom originated at least 150 years ago. Oral histories indicate that the parade may be even older.

Men and boys dress in white clothes, which fit in well with the snowy landscape. Around their hips and across their backs they hang a variety of noisemakers, including large, heavy bells. But the most impressive feature of the Glöcklerlauf costume is the huge, decorated headdress worn by each of the bell carriers. These amazing headdresses take months to create. A wooden frame in the shape of a flower, heart, pyramid, or star is covered with brightly colored silk or clear paper and decorated with fancy designs. These enormous "caps" weigh up to 60 pounds (27 kilograms) and sometimes exceed 10 feet (3 meters) in height.

When it is time for the Glöcklerlauf to begin, house lights, store lights, and street lights are turned off. The only light comes from the headdresses, which are illuminated from within by candles or flashlights. The participants look like large Chinese lanterns with legs. All night long the bell carriers parade through the darkened streets, admired by many of the people in the villages.

The Glöcklerlauf seems to have derived from an ancient pagan spring ritual. The lights are symbolic of the lengthening days of spring, and the bells and other noisemakers are designed to chase away the winter.

Some Austrian families keep their Christmas trees until the feast of Candlemas in early February. But in most homes, the tree is lit for the last time on January 6, the feast of the Epiphany, which brings the Twelve Nights to a close.

The Epiphany celebrates the arrival in Bethlehem of the *Drei Heiligen Könige*–the Three Holy Kings. One lovely, widespread Epiphany custom is *Sternsingen,* or star singing. Youngsters dress up as the Three Holy Kings, or Three Wise Men from the East, often with faces painted black, red, and white to represent different human races. The star singers go from house to house, led by children bearing torches and lanterns. They are followed by a "star carrier," who wears a flowing white garment and carries a shining star mounted on a long pole.

The Three Holy Kings stand majestically before each house, singing of their journey over desert sands and mountains on their way to bring their precious gifts to the newborn Christ child. The head of the household often invites the group inside for some refreshments. The children collect donations for charity before continuing on their journey. Once refreshed, the group proceeds to the next house with renewed enthusiasm.

With the passing of the Epiphany, the Advent and Christmas seasons have run full cycle. With its combination of Christian beliefs and secular legends, the period of the Twelve Nights retains a charm and magic that continues to be celebrated in modern times.

To celebrate the Epiphany, "star singers," children dressed as the Three Holy Kings, go from house to house to sing and collect donations for charity.

Skiers enjoy the slopes of the Austrian Alps during a Christmas holiday.

Alpine Holidays

The majestic Alps and their foothills stretch across the western, southern, and central parts of Austria, a country famous for some of the most beautiful scenery in the world. It would be difficult to exaggerate the magnetic attraction that the mountains have over the people of Austria. The Alps provide great pleasure to those who live on their forested slopes. After Christmas, many people from around the country take a vacation to the mountains to experience the joys of an Alpine holiday.

All over Austria, most schools and offices officially close from Christmas Eve through St. Stephen's Day, December 26. Some families take advantage of the time off and leave for a mountain holiday as soon as the Christmas Eve festivities are finished. For many people in Austria, Christmas would not be the same without a ride in a horse-drawn sleigh through the sparkling snow and pure, clear air of one of Austria's beautiful mountain retreats.

Many special events occur in the mountains and villages during the winter holiday season. At Innsbruck and nearby towns, high in the mountains of the Tyrol province, university students from all over the world participate in winter sports competitions in January. At several mountain resorts throughout Austria, guests are invited to greet the new year with hiking and skiing by torchlight. In Dornbirn, a city in the Vorarlberg province, the feast of the Epiphany, January 6, is celebrated each year with a toboggan race.

Austria has an amazing variety of local customs and festivals, developed in the seclusion of Alpine valleys and enriched by contact with people of other provinces. Many festivals, such as the Glöcklerlauf and Perchtenlauf, which are held during the Twelve Nights after Christmas, date back to a time before Christianity spread into central Europe.

In ancient times, villagers set food aside for the four elements—air, earth, fire, and water. The custom survives as the Twelve Nights begin on December 26 in certain parts of rural Austria, where farmers set down morsels of Christmas food at the roots of their fruit trees. The food is offered in hopes that the trees will bear fruit again during the coming year. Sleigh loads of feed are brought into the forests for the deer, so that even the wild animals can share the joys of Christmas.

Many Austrian families enjoy a mountain holiday after Christmas.

Another Alpine practice on the first night of the Twelve Nights is to collect the *Christwurz,* or Christmas rose, a plant that once was thought to be highly effective against the plague and other diseases.

Huge-horned straw figures called Schab *clear the way for the St. Nicholas Eve parade in the town of Bad Mittendorf.*

Church bells ring to chase off any demons that might be on the loose as the Twelve Nights begins.

The custom of lighting Christmas trees on graves is common in rural Austria. This custom may have arisen from the practice of lighting candles on graves on All Souls' Day to warm the shivering ghosts hovering nearby.

In many villages, mystery pageants or folk dramas present a variety of religious and *secular* (nonreligious) themes. The actors speak in regional dialects and wear traditional Alpine costumes.

Straw-clad characters are popular during the annual *Nikolospiel* performed in the town of Bad Mittendorf, in the Styria province. This combination parade and folk drama on December 5 heralds the arrival of Saint Nicholas, the patron saint of children. The crack of whips and clang of bells announce the beginning of the parade. Straw figures known as *Schab,* with huge horns on their heads, lead the procession into town and clear the streets for the parade. They are followed by an assortment of other characters, including a night watchman, a policeman, and a rider on a white horse. A person with a mask that bears smiling faces on all four sides carries a basket of sweets for the children.

The star of the parade, Saint Nicholas, is preceded by an angel, church caretakers with collection bags, and a "thunder bearer" carrying a large rod. Saint Nicholas is accompanied by a local priest and followed by a beggar and the scythe-wielding character of Death. Lucifer, with a three-pronged fork, is chained by two other devils and hounded by a Marriage-Devil and several Krampuses in artful masks. The Nicholas-hunter brings up the rear of the procession, keeping order among the Krampuses.

As the parade approaches, a large crowd of children gathers in the main room of one of the local inns. The rider on the white horse rides around in circles in front of the inn, attempting to drive away evil spirits. Inside the inn, it is very quiet, until the thunder bearer jumps into the room and frightens the children. The angel quickly expels him, and Saint Nicholas and the priest enter with a prayer: "Praise be to Jesus Christ."

Saint Nicholas gives a sermon, and the priest quizzes the children to see if they know their prayers. When they have recited their lessons to Saint Nicholas's satisfaction, the man with the smiling mask distributes sweets among the children.

The beggar begins a dialogue, but he is cut off in the middle by the figure of Death, swinging his scythe. Two Krampuses materialize at once to remove the body, and Saint Nicholas warns everyone in the room to take to heart what just happened.

When Saint Nicholas and the priest leave the inn, the room is free for the powers of darkness. Lucifer, the Marriage-Devil, and various other evil characters prance about wildly, creating a terrible commotion. Finally, the sound of the night watchman's horn signals the end of the play. The reign of the evil ones is at an end, and they storm outside to join the other participants in the Nikolospiel as the parade moves on to the next inn.

A considerably calmer rural Christmas custom is the tradition of "showing the Christ child." A church caretaker and two altar servers carry a *Weihnachtskrippe,* or Nativity scene, from house to house as they sing Christmas carols. They are followed by a group of children dressed as angels and shepherds. At each house, the children are invited inside to perform little Nativity plays. The householders reward the youngsters with Christmas cookies, hot chocolate, and other treats before sending them on to their next stop.

In one charming variation of this Christmas tradition, the family living farthest from the village church starts down from the mountain carrying the manger and caroling by torchlight. When they reach the first house on their route, the neighbor family comes out to join them. Family after family joins the procession until at last it reaches the steps of the church. There, a Nativity carol is sung and acted out: "Through the Darkness Gleams the Light." The entire village joins in the final chorus, which announces the birth of the Christ child.

A city lies nestled in the mountains of the Salzburg province.

The beauty and richness of these Alpine customs are carried on year after year by a people proud of their land and traditions. Their spirit and friendliness warm the snowy winter landscape, bringing a sense of joy and peace to the holiday season in the Austrian mountains.

The Vienna Boys' Choir sings during a "Christmas in Vienna" performance at the Vienna Konzerthaus.

"Silent Night"

Austria's heritage of Christmas music—in particular its lovely, melodic folk carols—is rare in its charm and beauty. The *Hirtenlieder*, or shepherd songs, have delighted Austrians for centuries. In these rustic tunes, sung in the broadest dialect, the singers imagine themselves in the company of the shepherds of Bethlehem, addressing the newborn Christ child and His parents in simple, affectionate words. Many of these songs contain refrains that imitate the sounds of shepherds' instruments. Here is an especially playful stanza from an old Tyrolean carol, "*Jetzt hat sich halt aufgetan das himmlische Tor*" ("The Gates of Heaven's Glory Did Spring Open Suddenly").

B ecause Austria's musical tradition is unusually rich and varied, Christmas carols for every mood echo from mountain villages and valley towns all through the holidays. Besides the shepherds' carols,

So came we running to the crib,
    I and also you,
A bee-line into Bethlehem,
    Hopsa, trala loo:
"O baby dear, take anything
    Of all the little gifts we bring:
Have apples or have butter,
    Maybe pears or yellow cheese;
Or would you rather have some nuts,
    Or plums, or what you please."
Alleluja, alleluja;
    Alle-, Alle-, Alleluja.

Although the original score for "Silent Night, Holy Night" vanished long ago, this is one of the oldest copies in existence.

there are companion carols, dance carols, lullaby carols, star carols, and those that can be performed properly only by yodeling.

In the early 1800's, almost every local church parish had its own poet, who added new songs to the Christmas treasury. From this tradition sprang the most famous of Austria's contributions to the celebration of Christmas—the beloved *"Stille Nacht, Heilige Nacht"* ("Silent Night, Holy Night").

Joseph Mohr wrote the words to "Silent Night, Holy Night" in 1816. At the time, Mohr was an assistant priest in Mariapfarr, a farming village southeast of Salzburg. The Napoleonic Wars were over, but Mariapfarr was still recovering from its occupation by French troops. This fact—as well as the majestic silence and beauty of a winter night—may have prompted Mohr to write the "Silent Night, Holy Night" lines.

In 1817, Mohr moved to Oberndorf, a town northwest of Salzburg, where he became assistant priest of St. Nicholas Church. The economy of Oberndorf was suffering because the Napoleonic Wars had caused the town's main source of income, the salt trade, to decline. The St. Nicholas Church organ was out of order, and the parishioners lacked funds to repair it. Mohr wanted something special to make up for the lack of organ music at the Christmas Eve midnight Mass.

Mohr took his poem to his friend Franz Xaver Gruber, a schoolteacher in the nearby village of Arnsdorf. Gruber also was the church organist at both Arnsdorf and Oberndorf. In 1818, Gruber composed the lyrical melody, so characteristic of Austrian folk music.

Both Gruber and Mohr were accomplished guitarists. In fact, they often entertained guests at local inns to supplement their meager salaries. Gruber brought his music to Mohr, and the two conducted a brief rehearsal with the St. Nicholas Church choir. "Silent Night, Holy Night" was performed for the first time at the Christmas Eve

midnight Mass in 1818. Mohr, a tenor, sang the melody. Gruber, a bass, sang harmony. The choir repeated the last two lines of each stanza in four-part harmony, and Mohr accompanied the voices on guitar.

The villagers were still talking about the simple, haunting strains of "Silent Night, Holy Night" the following spring, when Carl Mauracher, an organ builder from the Ziller Valley in the Tyrol province, came to repair the organ at St. Nicholas Church. Not much is known about what happened then, but Mauracher probably asked to hear the carol or to see a copy of the music. The authors evidently complied, perhaps even supplying Mauracher with the original musical composition.

Mauracher probably played a major role in spreading the carol's popularity. He must have taken the tune back to his native Ziller Valley—a good piece of luck, since the area was home to many traveling singers. From the Ziller Valley, the carol began its long voyage around the world.

On Christmas Eve in 1819, the first performance of "Silent Night, Holy Night" outside Oberndorf was sung by members of the Rainer family in the church of Fügen, a village in the Ziller Valley. Three years later, Austria's Emperor Francis I spent a few days in a castle

The Silent Night Memorial Chapel in the town of Oberndorf stands on the original site of St. Nicholas Church, where "Silent Night, Holy Night" was performed for the first time on Christmas Eve in 1818.

The grave of Joseph Mohr, who wrote the words to "Silent Night, Holy Night," lies in the town of Wagrein, where Mohr died.

near the village with Russia's Czar Alexander I. The Rainer family performed for the royal visitors. Among the tunes they sang was "Silent Night, Holy Night." The singers and their carol so enchanted the monarchs that the Rainers were invited to travel to Russia. From 1824 to 1838, the family toured Europe extensively.

Certain members of the family were responsible for introducing the carol to the United States. A group called the Rainer Quartet sang "Silent Night, Holy Night" before the Alexander Hamilton monument in New York City on Christmas Day in 1839. Joseph A. Rainer, a descendant of the Rainer family, devoted a great deal of energy to preserving the original melody.

Another singing group from the Ziller Valley also helped to spread "Silent Night, Holy Night." Upon Mauracher's return from Oberndorf, the organ builder taught the song to Caroline, Joseph, Andreas, and Amalie Strasser. Each year the Strasser children traveled to Leipzig in the kingdom of Saxony, the site of a giant annual trade fair. Their parents were glovemakers, and the children's job was to attract customers to their parents' display by singing Tyrolean folk tunes.

At one of the Strasser's performances, the director of music in the kingdom of Saxony overheard the Strasser children. He gave them tickets to one of the concerts that he regularly conducted in the guild house of the *drapers* (people who sell cloth) of Leipzig. The king and queen of Saxony also attended the concert. At the close of the performance, the director announced that in the audience were four children with the finest voices he had heard in years. The children then performed some of their folk melodies. Among the Strassers' collection of songs was the "Song from Heaven"—the children's name for "Silent Night, Holy Night." The carol so delighted the royal couple that they invited the children to perform it at the castle. On Dec. 24, 1832, the Strasser children sang "Silent Night, Holy Night" at the Royal Saxon Court Chapel in Pleissenburg Castle.

By 1838, the song appeared in the *Leipziger Gasangbuch*, and in 1840, it was printed in the *Catholic Hymn and Prayer Book*. In 1849, a modified version of the song appeared in *Devotional Harmony*, a Methodist compilation of songs printed in the United States.

The king of Prussia, Frederick William IV, heard the carol for the first time in 1854, when it was sung by the entire choir of the Royal Court Chapel in Berlin. It was not until that year that the Royal Court Chapel began to make inquiries as to who had actually written and composed the carol.

By the 1840's, "Silent Night, Holy Night" was being attributed to the Austrian composers Joseph Haydn, Wolfgang Amadeus Mozart, and a few others. Haydn's brother, Michael, had been a paying guest in the schoolhouse home of Franz Xaver Gruber, and many people believed that Michael Haydn must have composed the hymn.

On Dec. 30, 1854, Gruber wrote a letter to Berlin that set the record straight. By that time, Gruber was serving as an organist at the city church of Hallein, in the Salzburg province. His letter contained proof that he had composed the music for the words that were written by Joseph Mohr. Mohr had died in Wagrein, a town in the Salzburg province, on Dec. 4, 1848.

The old St. Nicholas Church no longer stands. But in the early 1900's, the town of Oberndorf commissioned a memorial to Mohr and Gruber. The Silent Night Memorial Chapel stands outside the new St. Nicholas Church. There are numerous portraits of Gruber, but not one likeness of the obscure priest who wrote the words. Mohr's body was exhumed from its grave in Wagrein, and his skull was sent to a sculptor in Vienna who attempted to create a sculpture of Mohr based on the shape of his skull. The sculptor mistakenly returned the skull to Oberndorf instead of to Wagrein. To this day, Mohr's skull rests beneath the Nativity scene in Oberndorf's Silent Night Memorial Chapel.

The small chapel that commemorates the carol's author and composer attracts thousands of pilgrims every year. Shaped like an octagon, the chapel features a beautifully carved altar and stained-glass windows dedicated to Mohr and Gruber.

A giant Christmas tree adorning the front of the Vienna City Hall is the focus of the city's Christmas market, which is generally thronged with shoppers.

Visions of Vienna

Vienna at Christmastime is a symphony for the senses. The sights, smells, sounds, tastes, and textures of the season combine in a happy whirl of excitement. Days are short—on Christmas Eve the sun does not rise until nearly 8 a.m., and it sets just after 4 p.m. A heavy layer of clouds often blocks the sun's warmth, and the temperature usually is below freezing. Still, during the holidays, the capital is cheerful. Vienna lights up like a Christmas tree. Thousands of colored lights, arranged in many different Christmas designs, twinkle and glitter along the main streets. Most Christmases in Vienna are white. Set like a jewel in the snowy landscape, the city looks exceptionally romantic.

On Christmas Eve, icicles hang from Vienna's roofs and windowsills. Pedestrians—wearing boots, down jackets, and long woolen scarves—exhale little puffs of steam, like old-fashioned locomotives. Every few blocks, the warm red glow of a chestnut vendor's stove attracts a group of last-minute shoppers. Paper cones of hot roasted chestnuts will tide them over until Christmas Eve dinner.

By early evening, most shops and restaurants have closed their doors, and many people are home preparing for the evening's festivities. After dinner and the exchange of gifts, the whole city eagerly

awaits the midnight bells that call the faithful to worship. It is hard to imagine Christmas Eve in Vienna without the deep, ringing booms and melodious tones that joyfully announce the birth of *Christkindl*, the Christ child.

Vienna is a musical city at any time of the year. But Christmas has special sounds that are unique to the season. The delightful street organs attract the city's children. Other melodious tunes include the *Turmblasen*, the Christmas music that trumpets forth from St. Stephen's Cathedral and the steeple of the Guildhall every Christmas Eve.

The angelic voices of the Vienna Boys' Choir traditionally ring out on Christmas Eve in the Burgkappelle at the Hofburg, formerly the private chapel of the Hofburg Castle in downtown Vienna. The choir also sings on Christmas Day and at services on St. Stephen's Day, December 26. Instrumentalists, as well as tenors and basses from the Vienna State Opera, supplement the boys' sopranos and altos. Very little has changed in the choir's performance since the chapel was built in the late 1400's—except, of course, that the youngsters have become famous all over the world.

The Austrian composers Joseph Haydn and Franz Schubert were members of the Vienna Boys' Choir, whose continued existence over a period of more than 500 years is another testament to the Austrian people's profound love of music. Christmas in Vienna would not be the same without this magnificent choir.

One of the most wonderful experiences to be had in Vienna at Christmastime is a visit to one of its many pastry shops. Demel's pastry shop, the world-famous *Konditorei*, or confectioner, offers a magnificent annual Christmas display. Gorgeous fairy-tale landscapes feature butter-cream meadows, chocolate Tyrolean cottages, *marzipan* (almond and sugar candy) glaciers, and delicious stylized Christmas trees. Even people who can't afford the calories or the expense of a *Schaumrolle* (pastry filled with whipped cream) or a *Doboschtorte* (rich, chocolate-filled cake with caramel topping) can feast their eyes on the displays for free.

Delicious Christmas treats fill the window of Demel's pastry shop, a Vienna landmark.

It is said that Demel's represents the Viennese *Lebensart*, the city's manner of living, and the city's sweet way of life. The shop is a national monument. Demel's uses only the finest ingredients from all over the world. The shop even mixes its own chocolate from selected cocao beans and sugar.

Ludwig Dehne, a sugar baker's apprentice from Württemberg, founded the pastry shop in 1786. He established the shop across from the stage door of the old Burg Theater. Dehne's beautifully crafted cookies, doughnuts, and ice cream creations became

A pastry chef decorates a Christmas cake at Vienna's Hotel Sacher.

Hundreds of elegantly dressed guests (opposite page) *dine in the grand banquet hall of the Hofburg palace during the Imperial Ball, one of the most glittering events in Vienna on New Year's Eve.*

favorites with the performers at the theater. Unfortunately, Dehne died before his wife became court caterer and his shop was named the official sugar bakery of the imperial household. The business left the family in 1857, when Christoph Demel bought the shop from the founder's grandson. In 1888, Demel moved the pastry shop to its current location in the *Kohlmarkt,* where it has landmark status.

New Year's would simply not be the same without the delightful melodies of Johann Strauss, Jr., the "Waltz King." The Vienna Philharmonic Orchestra helps celebrate the New Year with its annual all-Strauss concert of waltzes and polkas. Another beloved tradition is the annual New Year's Eve performance of the Strauss operetta *Die Fledermaus* by the Vienna State Opera. As people in Austria enjoy the richness of the holiday season, they do so to the tune of Strauss waltzes.

The most important event in Vienna on New Year's Eve is the Imperial Ball at the Hofburg. Hundreds of guests from around the world gather to celebrate the holiday in the tradition of the old Austrian monarchy. Everyone dresses formally—in white tie and tails and elegant ballgowns—and the musicians' costumes from the 1700's give the impression that the event is taking place in the time of Mozart.

Guests are greeted with cocktails, and ladies receive a memento from a woman dressed as the empress. Dinner is served in several halls while the costumed musicians play Strauss waltzes. After dinner, the guests gather in the main hall for the official New Year's celebration—a one-hour operetta with professional singers and dancers. The whole affair lasts until nearly four in the morning.

The Imperial Ball marks the beginning of *Fasching.* About seven weeks later, on Ash Wednesday, Fasching comes to an end. But glorious visions of Vienna play on in people's dreams.

Beautifully crafted
Weihnachstkrippen
(Nativity scenes),
like this one outside
Vienna's City Hall,
occupy a special place
in Austrian Christmas
celebrations.

Christmas Expressions

Austrian cattle farmers, shepherds, and villagers—the inhabitants of the country's secluded Alpine valleys—have created their own cultural expressions and entertainment. Their mountain isolation has encouraged a great variety of folk arts, from folk songs and poetry to woodworking.

No holiday has drawn a more enthusiastic response from Austria's talented folk artists than Christmas. The joy and wonder of the season perhaps are best expressed in the magnificent *Weihnachtskrippen* (Nativity scenes) that occupy a special place in almost every Austrian church and home during the Christmas holidays.

The Weihnachtskrippe seems to have originated in medieval Christmas plays and in the late Gothic Christmas altars inspired by these plays. The Christmas plays gave rise to the *Landschaftskrippe*, the most frequently seen type of Weihnachtskrippe in Austria. In the Landschaftskrippe, the Nativity scene is set into a landscape. Sometimes the Holy Family is sheltered in a cave, or occasionally they are amid the ruins of King David's castle, indicating Jesus's ancestry. Bethlehem may be portrayed as an East Asian settlement. But most often, the Holy Family is shown in a typical Austrian stable and village.

A live reenactment of the Nativity draws a crowd at a Christmas market in Vienna.

The movable figures of the Landschaftskrippe always include the Holy Family and usually a selection of angels, animals, and shepherds. The main figures often are dressed in the costumes of the Austrian province in which they were created. Minor characters may be clothed in more varied fashions.

Some of the more decorated Weihnachtskrippen feature dozens of figures, which are often engaged in activities having nothing to do with the Nativity itself. Hunters may chase deer through the mountains above Bethlehem. In the town, a cobbler is shown working with awl and twine, and a blacksmith is striking a hot iron. Soldiers costumed in uniforms from the 1700's stand at attention.

The *Kastenkrippe*, a form found mostly in the Salzkammergut area of central Austria, derives from late Gothic Christmas altars. Fixed figures appear on a landscape that rises steeply in the background. The Weihnachtskrippe is boxlike, with a glass window in front.

Old genuine Weihnachtskrippen are highly prized. A number of them have found their way into museums, including the Austrian Folklore Museum in Vienna and the Christmas Crib Museum in Saalfelden's Ritzen Castle.

The symbols of Christmas in the Weihnachtskrippen—carved angels and shepherds, handmade dolls and horses, paintings, delicate woodcuts, fancy ornaments, and delicious pastries—are created lovingly by Austrian artists and craftspeople. The beauty of these creations enhances the dancing, the faith, the family warmth, the music, and the traditions—all of which make Christmas in Austria so special.

Viennese Christmas and New Year's greetings

People began exchanging printed Christmas and New Year's greeting cards in the mid-1800's. At first, such cards were quite elaborate, but by the early 1900's, the inexpensive postcard became a much more popular way to remember distant relatives and friends during the holidays.

One of the most distinctive styles of Christmas postcards was developed by artists who belonged to a group called the *Wiener Werkstätte* (Vienna Workshops). The group was founded in

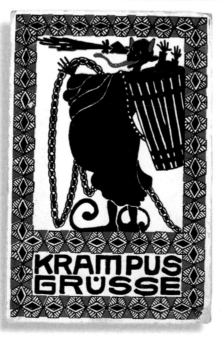

Images on Christmas postcards produced by the Wiener Werkstätte *in the early 1900's include a stylized Christmas tree* (above) *and the evil Krampus* (left), *complete with birch sticks and rattling chains. A New Year's card* (far left) *sends best wishes for 1917.*

1903 by artists Josef Hoffmann and Koloman Moser and funded by the industrialist Fritz Warndorfer. In time, more than 100 members joined the cooperative. They crafted ceramics, furniture, jewelry, and pottery, as well as fabrics, greeting cards, and posters. Art produced by the Wiener Werkstätte was characterized by simple shapes and geometric patterns. Yet, the products were designed for an exclusive audience and often commanded high prices. The Wiener Werkstätte closed in 1932 because of financial problems.

Christkindl is featured in Christmas postcards created from about 1907 to 1910 (left and below left). *A New Year's postcard from about 1910* (below) *includes such symbols of good luck as a pig, a horseshoe, a four-leaf clover, and a chimney sweep.*

Austrian Treats

Ischler Törtchen
(raspberry tartlets)

1/2 lb. plus 4 Tbsp. unsalted butter
(2 1/2 sticks)
2/3 cup sugar
2 cups all-purpose sifted flour
1 3/4 cups ground almonds
1/8 tsp. cinnamon
1/2 cup raspberry jam
confectioners' sugar

1. Cream the butter and sugar until light and fluffy. Add flour, 1/2 cup at a time, along with the cinnamon and almonds. Beat until mixture becomes a slightly stiff dough.

2. Shape the dough into a ball and wrap in plastic wrap. Refrigerate for 1/2 hour.

3. Divide the dough in half. On a lightly floured surface, roll out half of the dough to 1/8-inch thickness.

4. Using a 2 1/2-inch or 3-inch cookie cutter, cut as many circles from the dough as you can. Collect the scraps and roll the dough again, cutting more circles. You should have about 12. Place circles on an ungreased cookie sheet.

5. Roll out the remaining half of the dough, and cut out circles in the same way. But before arranging this second group of circles on a cookie sheet, cut out the center of each circle with a 1/2-inch cookie cutter.

6. Bake both groups of circles at 325 °F for 10–13 minutes or until lightly browned. With a metal spatula, gently ease the cookies onto a wire rack and allow to cool.

To assemble:

7. Spread raspberry jam on each circle.

8. Dust the cut-out cookies with confectioners' sugar. Then place one cut-out cookie on top of each jam-coated solid cookie. Press gently.

Yield: 12 tartlets.

Stollen (Christmas bread)

2 packages dry yeast

1/4 cup very warm water (110 °F)

3/4 cup milk at room temperature or slightly warmed

1/2 cup sugar

1/2 tsp. salt

1/2 cup unsalted butter, softened

2 large eggs plus 1 additional egg yolk, lightly beaten together

4 3/4 cups all-purpose sifted flour

1 cup raisins or currants (or a 1-cup mixture of both)

1/2 cup diced citron

1/2 cup diced candied orange peel or other candied fruit

3/4 cup chopped blanched almonds

2 tsp. cinnamon

1/2 cup confectioners' sugar for dusting

1. Mix yeast with the water and stir to dissolve.

2. Add the milk, salt, sugar, butter, and the 2 whole eggs plus the yolk from the third egg. Blend well.

3. Dust the raisins (or currants), citron, and candied orange peel (or candied fruit) with a little of the flour, and then add the almonds. Mix in the cinnamon, and set fruit and nut mixture aside.

4. Add half the flour to the yeast mixture and stir until smooth. Cover and let rise in a warm place until doubled in size—about 1 hour.

5. Add the remaining flour and knead until smooth and elastic—about 5 minutes. Knead in the fruit and nut mixture. Place the dough in an oiled bowl, turning the dough so it is completely coated. Cover and let rise for about 30 minutes.

6. Divide the dough into 2 equal portions. Press 1 portion of the dough into a large flat circle. Fold 1 side of the circle of dough over so that the top half is 1 inch from the edge of the bottom half, forming a split loaf shape. Repeat this step with the remaining portion of dough.

7. Place each loaf on a greased baking sheet, cover with plastic wrap, and let rise again until doubled in size—about 30 minutes. Bake at 375 °F for 40 minutes until golden brown.

8. Cool on wire rack. Sprinkle top generously with confectioners' sugar before serving.

Yield: 2 loaves.

1. Preheat oven to 350 °F. Line large cookie sheet with aluminum foil.

2. Beat egg whites until foamy. Add cream of tartar and continue beating until stiff.

3. Gradually add sugar—1 tablespoon at a time—beating after each addition. Beat at high speed 3 minutes after last addition.

Spanishche Windbäckerei (Spanish Wind meringue cookies)

4 egg whites (1/2 cup)
1/4 tsp. cream of tartar
3/4 cup sugar

4. Pipe batter into the form of small wreaths on cookie sheet, using pastry bag fitted with open star tube. Sprinkle with decorating crystals.

5. Place in preheated oven and immediately turn off heat. Leave in oven overnight. Do *not* open oven door during this time.

   These cookies are beautiful tied with ribbons to the Christmas tree.

   Yield: about 3-5 dozen cookies, depending on size.

Kletzenbrot (Christmas fruit bread)

3 cups sifted flour
2/3 cup brown sugar
3 tsp. baking powder
2 tsp. baking soda
1/4 tsp. salt
2 cups buttermilk
1 cup chopped nuts
1 cup chopped prunes
1 cup diced dates or figs
1 cup raisins

1. Blend all dry ingredients together. Add buttermilk slowly, stirring to make a smooth dough.

2. Stir in nuts and fruits.

3. Grease and flour a 10-inch tube pan. Spoon batter into pan.

4. Bake at 350 °F for 45 minutes.

   Yield: 1 loaf.

Pfeffernüsse (peppernut cookies)

3 cups all-purpose sifted flour
1 tsp. cinnamon
1/8 tsp. cloves
1/4 tsp. white pepper
3 eggs
1 cup sugar
1/3 cup very finely chopped blanched almonds
1/3 cup very finely chopped candied orange peel and citron

The secret of good "peppernuts" is to ripen the dough 2–3 days before baking and to store the cookies 1–2 weeks before eating.

1. Mix flour and spices and set aside.

2. Beat eggs until foamy and slowly add sugar. Continue beating until thick and lemon-colored. Slowly mix in flour, then almond, then orange peel and citron.

3. Wrap dough in foil and refrigerate for 2–3 days. When ready to bake, roll dough into 1-inch balls.

4. Space balls 2 inches apart on greased baking sheet.

5. Bake at 350 °F for 15–20 minutes. Cool on wire rack. Store in a covered container for 1–2 weeks.

6. Dredge cookies in confectioners' sugar before serving.

Yield: about 3 dozen cookies.

Topfenknödel (cheese dumplings)

15 oz. farmer cheese
4 eggs
1/4 tsp. salt
1/2 cup matzo meal
3 Tbsp. butter
1/2 cup fine bread crumbs

1. Mash the farmer cheese in a bowl using a potato masher. Still using the masher, add the eggs and salt. Gradually add the matzo meal. The dough will be quite firm. Chill for 2 hours.

2. Bring 3 quarts water to the simmering point. Form the mixture into dumplings 1 1/2 inches in diameter. Lower the dumplings into the simmering water and cook, uncovered, for 30 minutes or until dumplings rise to the surface and roll themselves over. (Do not stir.)

3. Remove dumplings one at a time using a slotted spoon and drain in a colander.

4. Melt the butter in a small saucepan. Add the bread crumbs and cook for 2–3 minutes until crumbs are crisp and lightly browned. Add the dumplings, cover the pan, and shake the pan back and forth over the heat until the dumplings are hot and coated with the toasted bread crumbs.

Serve Topfenknödel hot with jam or stewed fruit.

Yield: about 14–16 dumplings.

Faschingskrapfen (Carnival jelly doughnuts)

1/4 cup granulated sugar
1 cup warm milk (110 °F)
2 packages dry yeast
4 cups all-purpose sifted flour
1/2 tsp. salt
2 to 3 Tbsp. oil
2 egg yolks
1/2 cup jam
oil for deep frying
confectioners' sugar for dusting

1. Stir 1 teaspoon of the granulated sugar into the warm milk and sprinkle yeast over milk. Let stand for 5 minutes or until the surface is frothy.

2. Blend flour, remaining granulated sugar, and salt in a large bowl and set aside.

3. In a medium bowl, blend the oil and egg yolks. Add the yeast mixture.

4. Pour egg and yeast mixture into flour mixture and beat until a stiff dough forms. Cover and let rise for 20 minutes in a warm place.

5. On a floured surface, roll out the dough to a 1/2-inch thickness. Cut out 3-inch rounds.

6. Place a teaspoon of jam in the center of a round, and carefully place another round on top. Press edges firmly together. Using a 2 1/2-inch round cookie cutter, press down on dough to seal edges. Remove scraps and cut additional rounds.

7. Cover with a towel and let rise for about 30 minutes until rather plump.

8. Heat the oil to 360 °F in a deep pot with a lid. Place doughnuts, smooth topside down, into the hot oil. Cover and cook 2 to 3 minutes until golden brown. Turn them over and fry, uncovered, until golden brown. Drain on paper towels and dust with confectioners' sugar.

Note: Be sure to use enough oil so that the doughnuts can "swim" in the oil. This will produce the pale band around the middle that is distinctive to Faschingskrapfen.

Faschingskrapfen are best when eaten immediately, when they are warm and very fresh.

Yield: about 1 dozen doughnuts.

Austrian Crafts

Christkindl (Christ child ornament)

Assemble:

20-inch wooden doll form (from a crafts supplies store) or a round wooden clothespin

6-inch by 2-inch piece of gauze bandage

4 1/4-inch by 6-inch piece of cotton fabric with small print

25-inch piece of colored cotton cord to match fabric

fine-tip felt marking pen

pinking shears to cut fabric

1. Draw a face on the head of the doll form or clothespin with marking pen.

2. Wrap the wooden figure in the gauze. Starting with the head, cover all of the head and body except the face.

3. Lay the piece of fabric on a table, with the wrong side of the fabric facing up. Place the gauze-wrapped figure lengthwise at the center of one 4 3/4-inch end of the fabric. The figure should be lying facedown, with the head hanging over the end of the fabric. Fold both sides of the cloth around the figure so it is in a tube of cloth from the neck down.

4. Fold the bottom of the tube of fabric up behind the figure's head.

5. Wrap the cord around figure and cloth to secure the figure in the cloth. Knot the cord in back of the neck. Make a second knot at the ends of the cord to form a loop.

This ornament may be hung on the Christmas tree or placed in a cradle in a manger scene.

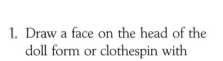

1. & 2.

3.

4.

5.

Back view

Front view

Glücksbringer Schwein aus Marzipan ("Good luck" marzipan pigs)

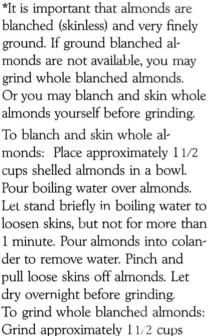

Ingredients:

1 cup finely ground blanched (skinless) almonds*

1 cup confectioners' sugar

1 egg white, unbeaten

a few drops of rosewater (or water if rosewater is not available)

red food coloring

Assemble:

bowl

pastry brush

wax paper

rolling pin

table knife

*It is important that almonds are blanched (skinless) and very finely ground. If ground blanched almonds are not available, you may grind whole blanched almonds. Or you may blanch and skin whole almonds yourself before grinding.

To blanch and skin whole almonds: Place approximately 1 1/2 cups shelled almonds in a bowl. Pour boiling water over almonds. Let stand briefly in boiling water to loosen skins, but not for more than 1 minute. Pour almonds into colander to remove water. Pinch and pull loose skins off almonds. Let dry overnight before grinding. To grind whole blanched almonds: Grind approximately 1 1/2 cups whole blanched almonds very fine, using a blender, coffee grinder, or hand grinder.

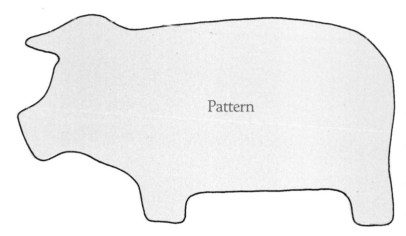

Pattern

1. To make marzipan dough, combine 1 cup ground blanched almonds and 1 cup confectioners' sugar in a bowl. Add the unbeaten white of 1 egg and a few drops of rosewater (or plain water). Sprinkle hands with confectioners' sugar to prevent sticking. Knead the mixture to make a smooth dough.

2. Roll out the dough between 2 sheets of wax paper to about 1/4-inch thickness.

3. Using a table knife, draw the outline of a pig in the dough. (Or you may make a paper pattern from the drawing provided and use the pattern to cut out the pigs.) Pull away the excess dough and save to make other pigs.

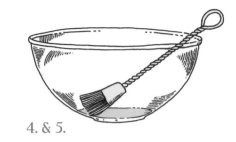

4. & 5.

4. Use small pieces of dough to shape ears, eyes, and tail. Lightly draw in mouth with knife.

5. Let pigs harden for 24 hours. Then use pastry brush to paint the pigs pink, using red food coloring diluted with water.

Yield: 6 pigs (approximately 4 inches by 2 inches)

These marzipan pigs may be eaten or used for decoration at New Year's celebrations. Or if you'd like to follow the Austrian tradition, give them to friends as Glücksbringer, to wish them good luck in the New Year.

Sun and moon ornaments

Assemble:

Yellow poster board

1/4-inch-wide flat braided or woven straw or flattened paper drinking straws or natural broom straw

Jar lid (about 2 1/4 inches across)

Scissors

Pencil

White glue

Cotton-tipped swabs

2 8-inch pieces of heavy gold or red cord

fine-tip felt marking pen

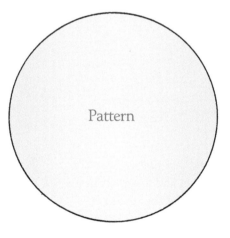

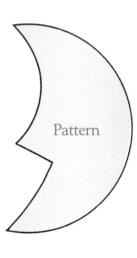

Pattern   Pattern

1. From the yellow poster board, cut out 2 circles for the sun and 2 crescents (about 3/5 circles) for the moon. Use the jar lid as a circle pattern. (Or make paper patterns for the sun and moon from the drawings provided.)

2. Cut straw in 1-inch pieces—about 26 pieces for the sun and 13 pieces for the moon.

3. Attach 1-inch pieces of straw braid (or straws) around the edge of each ornament as follows: Cover the inside of 1 sun circle with a light coat of glue, using fingers or cotton-

tipped swabs. Also apply glue to about 1/4-inch of the end of each piece of straw. Press each straw down firmly on the glued side of the sun circle so that 1/4 inch of each straw is on the sun and the rest extends beyond the edge. Continue attaching straw pieces (about 26) until the outer edge is filled. Straw pieces should fan out like rays of light. Then attach straw pieces to one moon crescent in the same manner, applying glue to the inside of the crescent and attaching about 13 straw pieces to the outside edge.

1. – 4.

4. Take an 8-inch piece of cord and cover about 1/2 inch of each end with glue. Press both ends of the cord together. Then press both ends onto the straw-filled inside of the sun circle. Position cord ends at the top of the ornament so the cord can be used as a loop for hanging. Attach the other 8-inch cord to the straw-filled inside of the moon crescent in the same manner. Make sure the cords and straws are firmly in place.

5. Cover the inside of the matching sun circle with glue. Align the 2 circles, inside to inside, and press firmly together. Glue the 2 moon crescents together in the same manner. Put ornaments under a heavy book or other weight for at least 15 minutes to dry.

6. If desired, use a fine-tip felt marking pen to draw a face on one or both sides of each ornament.

Hang the sun and moon ornaments on the Christmas tree to add a traditional Austrian touch.

5. & 6.

Patterns**

Angel

Assemble:

6-inch wooden doll form (from a crafts supplies store) or a round wooden clothespin, large size.

Gold, silver, and blue foil paper*

Gold stars with adhesive backs

18-gauge copper wire, 10 1/2 inches long

2 natural-color pre-drilled wooden beads, about 7/16-inch in diameter

white glue

needle and quilting thread or other strong thread

fine-tip felt marking pen

scissors

ruler

pencil

*If colored heavy foil-sided paper is not available, foil gift-wrap or construction paper may be substituted.

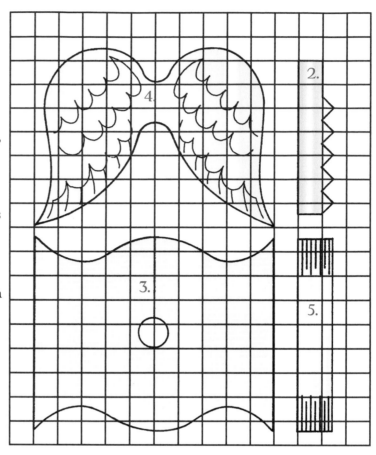

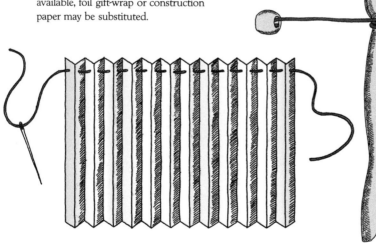

First assemble each part of the angel, following the instructions in steps 1–6.

1. Skirt: Cut out a 6-inch by 12-inch piece of gold foil paper. Make a 6-inch-high skirt by pleating the foil in 1/2-inch folds. With the pleats folded together, use needle to run an 18-inch-long thread through pleats at top of skirt.

2. Crown: Cut a 3 1/2-inch by 3/4-inch piece of gold foil paper. Cut points (about 1/4-inch deep and 1/2-inch wide) across 2 1/2 inches of the crown. Then cut a 1/4-inch-deep strip off the remaining 1 inch (on same side as points).

3. Top of gown: Cut a 5-inch by 4-inch piece of blue foil paper Cut out a circle (5/8-inch in diameter) in the center. Then make a cut from that circle to the middle of one of the 5-inch-long sides. Cut curved edge along both 5-inch-long sides as shown. Cover the foil side with adhesive gold stars.

4. Wings: Cut two 5-inch by 3 3/4-inch pieces of silver foil paper. Glue the two pieces back-to-back to form a piece that is silver on both sides. Cut to shape a pair of wings (as shown). If desired, lightly draw in feathers with a pencil.

5. Hair: Cut a 4-inch by 3/4-inch piece of silver foil paper. Make cuts about 3/4-inch deep into each end to form fringes.

6. Arms: Place the doll form or clothespin in the center of the copper wire. Wind each end of the wire once around the doll form at the neck. Fold back each end of wire about 1/2 inch. Slip a wooden bead onto bent part of wire at each end so bead fits snugly.

Now put the parts of the angel together, following the instructions in steps 7–12.

7. Glue the hair onto the head of the doll form or clothespin. Roll fringed ends around a pencil so that hair curls up.

8. Put the skirt around the figure and tie the threads at the back of the neck. Glue together the last folds on each side of the skirt.

9. Place top of gown over arms and around neck of figure, slit side at the back. Use gold stars or glue to connect the two sides of back of gown top. Roll both sides of gown top down over arm, and attach front and back of gown top under the hands with a little glue.

10. Glue the crown on top of the head.

11. Glue the wings to the back of the gown top or to the back of the head, as desired.

12. Draw on face with marking pen.

The angel is ready to stand on a table or mantel or to put on top of a Christmas tree.

**Patterns shown are 1/2 actual size (shown on graph paper with 1/4-inch squares). To double size of patterns, draw same shapes on paper with 1/2-inch squares.

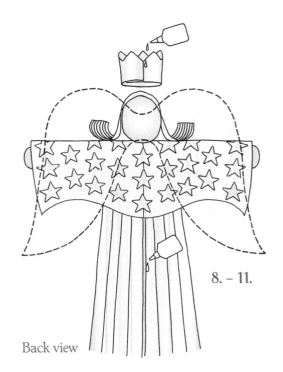

8. – 11.

Back view

Front view

Austrian Melodies

Silent Night, Holy Night

(Stille Nacht, Heilige Nacht)

Joseph Mohr, Franz Gruber, 1818

Translation: Anonymous, from C.L.
Hutchin's Sunday School Hymnal, 1871

2. Stille Nacht, heilige Nacht!
   Hirten erst kundgemacht!
   Durch der Engel Halleluja
   Tönt es laut von fern und nah:
   Christ, der Retter, ist da,
   Christ, der Retter, ist da!

3. Stille Nacht, heilige Nacht!
   Gottes Sohn, O, wie lacht
   Lieb aus deinem göttlichen Mund,
   Da uns schlägt die rettende Stund,
   Christ, in deiner Geburt,
   Christ, in deiner Geburt.

2. Silent night, holy night
   Shepherds quake at the sight;
   Glories stream from heaven afar,
   Heavenly hosts sing alleluia,
   Christ, the Savior, is born!
   Christ, the Savior, is born!

3. Silent night, holy night,
   Son of God, love's pure light
   Radiant beams from Thy holy face,
   With the dawn of redeeming grace,
   Jesus, Lord, at Thy birth,
   Jesus, Lord, at Thy birth.

Still, Still, Still

Traditional Austrian
Salzburg melody, 1819

Andante molto sostenuto

1. Still,__ still,__ still, Weil's__ Kind - lein__schla - fen__ will! Ma -
1. Still,__ still,__ still, He__ sleeps this__night so __ chill! The

ri - a __ tut es nie - der__sin - gen, Ih - re __ keu - sche Brust dar - brin - gen,
Vir - gin's__ten - der arms en - fold - ing, Warm and__safe the Child are__hold - ing,

Still,__ still,__ still, Weil __ Kind - lein __ schla - fen __ will.
Still,__ still,__ still, He __ sleeps this __ night so __ chill.

2. Schlaf, schlaf, schlaf,
   Mein liabes Kindlein, schlaf!
   Die Engel tuan schö musizieren,
   Bei dem Kindlein jubilieren,
   Schlaf, schlaf, schlaf,
   Mein liabes Kindlein, schlaf!

2. Sleep, sleep, sleep,
   He lies in slumber deep
   While angel hosts from heav'n
       come winging,
   Sweetest songs of joy are singing,
   Sleep, sleep, sleep,
   He lies in slumber deep.

Acknowledgments

Cover: © Soundsnaps/Shutterstock;
(inset) © Oliver Benn, Alamy Images
(back cover) © Andrzej Gibasiewicz,
Shutterstock

2: © De Agostini/Getty Images
6: © The Travel Library/Rex USA
7: © Herwig Prammer, Reuters/Landov
9: © Giovanni Simeone, SIME/4Corners Images
10: © Owen Franken, Corbis
11: © Maxine Hesse, Fotomax
13: © Austrian Archives/Corbis
15: © Bob Krist, Corbis
16: © Fantuz Olimpio, SIME/4Corners Images
17: © Vaccaro, Louis Mercier
18: AP/Wide World
19: © Ben Fink, FoodPix/Jupiter Images
20: © Hans Huber, Westend61/Alamy Images
21: © Sean Nel, Shutterstock
23: Austrian National Tourist Office
24: Austrian National Tourist Office
26: WORLD BOOK photo by Robert Frerck*
29: Fremdenverkehrsverband für Wien
30: © Walter Geiersperger, Corbis
32: © nagelestock.com/Alamy Images
33: © Hermann Danzmayr, Shutterstock
36: AP/Wide World
37: © Marc Garanger, Corbis
38: Fremdenverkehrsverband für Wien
40: Austrian National Tourist Office
41: © Roland Syba, Shutterstock
42: © Milan Ljubisavljevic, Shutterstock
43: © Leo Himsl, IGG Digital Graphic Productions GmbH/Alamy Images
44: © Helmut Kain
46: © Paul Trummer, The Image Bank/Getty Images

48: The Vienna Boys' Choir
49: © Joe Klamar, AFP/Getty Images
50: © Bavaria-Verlag
51: © Joe Klamar, AFP/Getty Images
53: © Hulton Archive/Getty Images
54: © Harald A. Jahn, allOver
55: © Hermann Danzmayr, Shutterstock
56: © Irek, 4Corners Images
57: © Duncan Smith
58: © Laif, Aurora
59: © Bob Krist, Corbis
60: © Harald A. Jahn, allOver
61: © Hulton Archive/Getty Images
62: © Eye Ubiquitous/Hutchison
63: © Hulton Archive/Getty Images
64: © Austrian Archives/Corbis; © Hulton Archive/Getty Images; © Austrian Archives/Corbis
Advent Calendar: © Giovanni Simeone, SIME/4Corners Images

Advent Calendar art: Eileen Mueller Neill*

Recipe Cards: Eileen Mueller Neill*

Craft Illustrations: WORLD BOOK Illustration*

*All entries marked with an asterisk (*) denote illustrations created exclusively for World Book, Inc.